ALSO BY HENRY B. KANE

AND ILLUSTRATED WITH PHOTOGRAPHS BY THE AUTHOR

The Tale of the Whitefoot Mouse

The Tale of the Bullfrog

The Tale of the Promethea Moth

The Tale of the Crow

The Tale of the White-Faced Hornet

These are BORZOI BOOKS
published in New York
by ALFRED A. KNOPF

Thoreau's WALDEN

"*I went to the woods because I wished to live deliberately, to front only the essential facts of life, and see if I could not learn what it had to teach, and not, when I came to die, discover that I had not lived.*"

THOREAU'S
WALDEN

A Photographic Register

BY

HENRY BUGBEE KANE

With an introduction by BROOKS ATKINSON

NEW YORK : ALFRED A. KNOPF

1946

INTRODUCTION

To celebrate the one hundredth anniversary of Thoreau's experiment in housekeeping at Walden Pond, Henry B. Kane decided some time ago to photograph as many as possible of the things that delighted Thoreau and nourished his spirit. Since nature does not change much in a century of New England living, Mr. Kane thought of portraying *Walden* as a contemporary book. By and large the natural wealth of the Walden region is identical with the richness Thoreau stored in his literary treasure chest. To people of literal minds Mr. Kane's project might seem like a perversion of the facts. For Walden Pond is now a public park where people swim, boat, fish, and picnic in astonishing numbers. The solitude that Thoreau prized has disappeared. But the people who enjoy a holiday beside the water have not changed the contours of the pond, blighted the flowers of the Concord countryside, nor driven off the animals and birds.

Even now the pond freezes when the winter settles down and melts when the sun comes north in the spring. Living in the town of Lincoln only two miles away, Mr. Kane is a neighbor of Walden Pond and can keep Thoreau's inland sea under observation. He notes that the bluebirds, redwings, and song sparrows reach the Concord region in mid-March, as they did in Thoreau's day. In the spring of 1845, when Thoreau was hewing the timbers for his house in the cove, the ice remained until the first of April. Early spring in New England in 1945 was abnormally warm; Walden was free of ice on the night of March 20. Thoreau would have liked to record that early date. But it brings our time close to his, or his close to ours, to remember that the second year of his Walden adventure was also an early spring: Walden was first completely open on March 25; and in 1852, when he was still writing his testament to Walden, the pond was open on March 23. The principles and habits of nature have not changed much in one hundred years.

All of us would be delighted if it were possible to photograph the little house that Thoreau built with his own hands and occupied for two years. That would be the most dramatic memorial there could be to Thoreau, particularly if the house still stood where he built it. But the house was trundled away during Thoreau's lifetime, I believe, to serve less glorious uses in a barnyard. The trees have changed around that spot. But it is a little difficult to know just what they were like when Thoreau was living there. May Alcott drew a sketch of the house embowered in trees on a little hill above the pond. According to a rude wood engraving made from memory in 1880 the house stood, not among trees, but in an unkempt, fenced-off clearing. On the titlepage of the first edition, published in 1854, the house is crowded and dwarfed by black fir trees. But to judge by Thoreau's own description, none of these representations is wholly accurate. " My house was on the side of a hill," he wrote, " immediately on the edge of the larger wood, in the midst of a young forest of pitch pines and hickories, and half a dozen rods from the pond, to which a narrow footpath led down the hill." Sumac grew luxuriantly around the house. The young pitch pines rubbed and creaked against the shingles. On the evidence of the flowers, bushes, and scrub-oak that Thoreau said grew in his dooryard there seems to have been some sort of clearing, with pitch pines beginning to establish new dominion. Probably the forest has changed more than any other aspect of nature beside the cove where Thoreau lived, and the pine forests here photographed are richer. Before the New England hurricane of 1938 the trees around Walden must have been more luxuriant than those Thoreau lived under. Partly as a result of his devotion to nature, trees are everywhere more reverenced today than they were a hundred years ago.

It seems reasonable to suppose that the pond has not changed, and that what Mr. Kane has photographed Thoreau saw when he lived there. Thoreau was in love with the pond. He watched the surface closely in all lights and under all conditions — marveling at it when it was placid, delighting in it when it rained, admiring it when the wind set it in motion. The ripples made him dream of cosmological themes. By watching the pond for the proper light and surface conditions, and perhaps dropping a pebble into the water to make rings of ripples, Mr. Kane has recaptured for us the little lovelinesses that Thoreau was fond of. Nor have the flowers or berries lost luster in a hundred years. The photographer has understood the tenderness of growing things.

Before the geese get into the air they furiously splash the surface of the water as Thoreau reported and Mr. Kane confirms. Sitting at his window in the winter, Thoreau must have seen many chickadees plumping down for a bite to eat like the one pictured in this book. Since his eyes and mind were not so fast as the lens of the camera, Thoreau may never have known how comic this friendly little bird can look when he is rushing to breakfast.

The brilliant snow pictures bring me closest to Thoreau. What Mr. Kane has seen in the Concord region is exactly what Thoreau saw when he walked through the snow and kept his appointments with trees he liked in Concord and Lincoln. The magic of snow has been going on without interruption all these years. Since the day of the hermitage, Walden has weathered thousands of snowstorms that have maculated the limbs and plastered the trunks of trees with whiteness; and as soon as the skies cleared, the mice, squirrels, and rabbits have continued to draw their traceries across the snow with innocent dexterity. These pictures re-create the winter's tales that *Walden* contains. One of the best photographs shows granulated snow, no longer fresh, melting and evaporating in the spring. That photograph overflows with seasonal atmosphere; just beyond the range of the camera Thoreau hovers around it. When winter was relenting, spring was expanding, and the green was coming up from beneath the cold whiteness, Thoreau always rejoiced to be there to see the season change. Particularly in his last year, when he could not get about freely out of doors, he would have cherished that photograph for the skill with which it has caught one recurring episode in the timeless rhythm of nature.

Anyone can see at a glance that Mr. Kane has enjoyed making these images of Thoreau's Walden. Chiefly on Saturdays and Sundays, when he could leave his desk at the Massachusetts Institute of Technology, he has ranged the Walden country in search of the things that impressed Thoreau. To be ready with his camera at the right moment, to make use of the snow when it was fresh and the light perfect, to photograph the lady's-slippers when they were at the height of their beauty — he has had to keep his mission constantly in the back of his mind. He has had to watch the sun and the clouds so that he could catch them in conjunction. He has had to be ready with his camera the instant the geese started to splash. In general, he has had to have some of Thoreau's faith in the importance of what he was doing.

He has also had to be versatile about his subjects — particularly the wild ones. The screech owl is one that flew into his garage and had to submit to photography. The horned owl is the grown version of one he took from a nest and brought up by hand for months to serve as a model. After searching the fields he was lucky to find one partridge who stuck to her nest until he had finished making pictures. To show the chickadee on the wing he made dozens of photographs near a feeding tray where he could set up his camera and catch a bird in focus by the hit-and-miss method. The woodchuck is one he captured in the field and took home. The skunk is one that slipped into a neighbor's cellar, where he became extremely unpopular. To help a neighbor and at the same time to get a good model, Mr. Kane managed to seize the skunk by the tail, which rendered it temporarily harmless, and took it home where he could make pictures with uncertain impunity.

In photographing the pond he had to use considerable ingenuity to avoid the bathhouses and boathouses and other park installations that were not there when Thoreau was in residence. But even before Walden was a public park it was a difficult pond to depict in one comprehensive photograph. For Walden cannot be easily assimilated; Thoreau pointed that out with a kind of romantic servility. One must serve it patiently, study its properties, respond to its moods, believe in its holiness. That is what Mr. Kane has been doing. Although he may think he has finished his work at Walden, he may be surprised to find himself working at it for years in an effort to recover the genius of the modest New England pond that Thoreau transfigured into one of the great bodies of water of the world. Thousands of thoughtful people in all countries know Walden more intimately than they know the Atlantic or Pacific ocean. One hundred years after Thoreau chose Walden as a seat of learning Mr. Kane is reminding us that the courses of instruction are still the same.

BROOKS ATKINSON

New York City

PREFACE

"Suffice it to say, that though bodily I have been a member of Harvard University, heart and soul I have been far away among the scenes of my boyhood. Those hours that should have been devoted to study, have been spent in scouring the woods, and exploring the lakes and streams of my native village."

(From Thoreau's entry in the Harvard Class Book, 1837)

Henry David Thoreau was the product of a small Massachusetts town. Of all the Concord intellectuals, — Emerson, Alcott, Channing, Hawthorne, — he alone could claim that town as his birthplace, and his entire life, except for rare and relatively short journeys, was spent within its borders.

Thoreau loved Concord, not the streets and houses of the village but its woods, its fields, its streams, its lakes and ponds. He knew its rivers better than the musquash hunters who took their living from those waters; knew the wood lots better than the farmers who held paper title to them. The things that most men saw with half an eye or not at all, were sharp and clear to him. Emerson said, "His power of observation seemed to indicate additional senses. He saw as with microscope, heard as with ear-trumpet, and his memory was a photographic register of all he saw and heard."

Much has been written of the influence of his contemporaries on Thoreau. Theirs was great. So too was that of the Greek, the Chinese, and the Hindu philosophers of antiquity. He was deeply concerned over fundamental problems, — slavery, economics, civil disobedience, universal simplification. He was writer, philosopher, surveyor, pencil maker, teacher, lecturer. Yet above all else he was a naturalist. From earliest boyhood until death, his love for nature colored everything he did and wrote and thought, nature as he knew it in Concord.

Walden is Thoreau's most important and mature work. It is also his best known. He went in 1845 to Walden, the Concord pond whose southern shores touch the Lincoln town line. There, in Emerson's woods, he built a cabin, and for the next two years lived the kind of life he had always longed for. He wrote his journal, rewrote earlier entries, hoed beans, and in the clouds, the dawn, the flight of birds, the battling of ants, saw teachings not visible to lesser men. He lived "as deliberately as Nature," and in that living found truths which have become ever more important with the passage of time, truths which today place him in the forefront not only of the sages of Concord but of all American philosophers.

What was this Walden country? How did it look? What were the scenes, the skies, the birds and animals, that Thoreau knew? If we could see them, we might gain greater insight into his nature, might have a better background for understanding this man who, during his own lifetime, was so little understood. Here, in the pages that follow, are those scenes. The years may have brought difference of detail, — the blades of grass are not the blades he saw, yet they are the same. This "photographic register of all he saw and heard" is Walden, the Walden of Thoreau, the Walden which was already in existence " on that spring morning when Adam and Eve were driven out of Eden."

HENRY B. KANE

Lincoln, Massachusetts
Spring, 1946

Thoreau's WALDEN

"Near the end of March, 1845, I borrowed an axe and went down to the woods by Walden Pond, nearest to where I intended to build my house. . . The ice in the pond was not yet dissolved, though there were some open spaces, and it was all dark-colored and saturated with water."

"There was never yet such a storm but it was Aeolian music to a healthy and innocent ear."

"Perhaps on that spring morning when Adam and Eve were driven out of Eden Walden Pond was already in existence . . ."

"There can be no very black melancholy to him who lives in the midst of nature and has his senses still."

[9]

"For the most part, I minded not how the hours went. . . . This was sheer idleness to my fellow-townsmen, no doubt; but if the birds and flowers had tried me by their standard, I should not have been found wanting."

"My 'best' room . . . my withdrawing room, always ready for company, on whose carpet the sun rarely fell, was the pine wood behind my house. Thither in summer days, when distinguished guests came, I took them, and a priceless domestic swept the floor and dusted the furniture and kept things in order."

"Some have been puzzled to tell how the shore became so regularly paved. . . . If the name was not derived from that of some English locality — Saffron Walden, for instance — one might suppose that it was called originally Walled-in Pond."

"I have frequently seen a poet withdraw, having enjoyed the most valuable part of a farm, while the crusty farmer supposed that he had got a few wild apples only. Why, the owner does not know it for many years when a poet has put his farm in rhyme, the most admirable kind of invisible fence . . ."

". . . the beech, which has so neat a bole . . . perfect in all its details . . . supposed by some to have been planted by the pigeons that were once baited with beechnuts near by."

"The true harvest of my daily life is somewhat as intangible and indescribable as the tints of morning or evening. It is a little star-dust caught, a segment of the rainbow which I have clutched."

"Sky water. It needs no fence. . . . It is a mirror which no stone can crack, whose quicksilver will never wear off, whose gilding Nature continually repairs; no storms, no dust, can dim its surface ever fresh."

"I dug my cellar in the side of a hill sloping to the south, where a woodchuck had formerly dug his burrow . . ."

"My enemies are worms, cool days, and most of all woodchucks. The last have nibbled for me a quarter of an acre clean."

"Time is but the stream I go a-fishing in. I drink at it; but while I drink I see the sandy bottom and detect how shallow it is. . . . I would drink deeper; fish in the sky, whose bottom is pebbly with stars."

"For many years I was self-appointed inspector of snow-storms and rain-storms, and did my duty faithfully; surveyor, if not of highways, then of forest paths and all across-lot routes . . ."

"Flint's, or Sandy Pond, in Lincoln, our greatest lake and inland sea, lies about a mile east of Walden. . . . Flint's Pond! Such is the poverty of our nomenclature. . . . Rather let it be named from the fishes that swim in it, the wild fowl or quadrupeds which frequent it, the wild flowers which grow by its shores. . . ."

"Goose Pond, of small extent, is on my way to Flint's. . . . This is my lake country. . . . and night and day, year in and year out, they grind such grist as I carry to them."

"Passing a cornfield the other day, close by a hat and coat on a stake, I recognized the owner of the farm. He was only a little more weatherbeaten than when I saw him last."

"The real attractions of the Hollowell farm, to me, were . . . the hollow and lichen-covered apple trees, gnawed by rabbits, showing what kind of neighbors I should have."

"One night in the beginning of winter, before the pond froze over, about nine o'clock, I was startled by the loud honking of a goose, and, stepping to the door, heard the sound of their wings like a tempest in the woods as they flew low over my house."

"Meanwhile also came the chickadees in flocks . . . to pick a dinner out of my wood-pile, or the crumbs at my door, with faint flitting lisping notes, like the tinkling of icicles in the grass . . ."

"Signs were hung out on all sides to allure (the traveller); some to catch him by the appetite, as the tavern and victualling cellar; some by the fancy, as the dry goods store and the jeweller's; and others by the hair or the feet or the skirt, as the barber, the shoe-maker, or the tailor. . . . For the most part I escaped wonderfully from these dangers . . ."

"Every day or two I strolled to the village to hear some of the gossip which is incessantly going on there, circulating either from mouth to mouth, or from newspaper to newspaper, and which, taken in homoeopathic doses, was really as refreshing in its way as the rustle of leaves and the peeping of frogs."

"Simplify, simplify. . . . The nation itself, with all its so-called internal improvements, which, by the way are all external and superficial, is . . . an unwieldy and overgrown establishment . . . ruined by luxury and heedless expense . . . and the only cure for it . . . is in a rigid economy, a stern and more than Spartan simplicity of life and elevation of purpose."

"In my house we were so near that we could not begin to hear — we could not speak low enough to be heard; as when you throw two stones into calm water so near that they break each other's undulations."

". . . made my supper of huckleberries and blueberries on Fair Haven Hill . . . If you would know the flavor of huckleberries, ask the cow-boy or the partridge. It is a vulgar error to suppose that you have tasted huckleberries who never plucked them."

"In October I went a-graping to the river meadows, and loaded myself with clusters more precious for their beauty and fragrance than for food."

"Sometimes I rambled to pine groves, standing like temples, or like fleets at sea, full-rigged, with wavy boughs, and rippling with light, so soft and green and shady that the Druids would have forsaken their oaks to worship in them."

"Walden is blue at one time and green at another . . . Viewed from a hilltop it reflects the color of the sky; but near at hand it is of a yellowish tint next the shore where you can see the sand, then a light green, which gradually deepens to a uniform dark green in the body of the pond."

"I have been surprised to detect encircling the pond . . . a narrow shelf-like path in the steep hillside . . . as old probably as the race of man here, worn by the feet of aboriginal hunters, and still from time to time unwittingly trodden by the present occupants of the land."

"Occasionally . . . I joined some impatient companion who had been fishing on the pond since morning . . . and, after practising various kinds of
philosophy, had concluded commonly, by the time I arrived, that he belonged
to the ancient sect of Coenobites."

"When other birds are still, the screech owls take up the strain . . . It is no honest and blunt tu-wit tu-who of the poets, but, without jesting, a most solemn graveyard ditty, the mutual consolations of suicide lovers remembering the pangs and the delights of supernal love in the infernal groves."

"For sounds in winter nights, and often in winter days, I heard the forlorn but melodious note of a hooting owl indefinitely far; such a sound as the frozen earth would yield if struck with a suitable plectrum, the very lingua vernacula of Walden Wood . . ."

"This is a delicious evening, when the whole body is one sense, and imbibes delight through every pore. I go and come with a strange liberty in Nature, a part of herself. As I walk along the stony shore of the pond in my shirt-sleeves, . . . all the elements are unusually congenial to me."

"Our village life would stagnate if it were not for the unexplored forests and meadows which surround it. We need the tonic of wildness — to wade sometimes in marshes where the bittern and the meadow-hen lurk, and hear the booming of the snipe."

"What is a country without rabbits and partridges? They are among the most simple and indigenous animal products; ancient and venerable families known to antiquity as to modern times."

"The partridge and the rabbit are still sure to thrive, like true natives of the soil, whatever revolutions occur. . . . Our woods teem with them both, and around every swamp may be seen the partridge or rabbit walk, beset with twiggy fences and horse-hair snares, which some cow-boy tends."

"Still grows the vivacious lilac a generation after the door and lintel and the sill are gone . . . planted and tended once by children's hands, in front-yard plots — now standing by wallsides in retired pastures . . . the last of that stirp, sole survivor of that family."

"Ere long . . . on every hill and plain and in every hollow, the frost comes out of the ground like a dormant quadruped from its burrow, and seeks the sea with music, or migrates to other climes in clouds. Thaw with his gentle persuasion is more powerful than Thor with his hammer."

"Sometimes I rambled . . . to swamps where the usnea lichen hangs in festoons from the white spruce trees, and toadstools, round tables of the swamp gods, cover the ground . . . the red alder berry glows like eyes of imps. . . ."

"The finest qualities of our nature, like the bloom on fruits, can be preserved only by the most delicate handling. Yet we do not treat ourselves nor one another thus tenderly."

"Sometimes, on Sundays, I heard the bells, the Lincoln, Acton, Bedford, or Concord bell, when the wind was favorable, a faint, sweet, and, as it were, natural melody, worth importing into the wilderness."

"I was even accustomed to make an irruption into some houses, where I was well entertained, and after learning the kernels and very last sieveful of news. . . . I was let out through the rear avenues, and so escaped to the woods again."

"Only that day dawns to which we are awake. There is more day to dawn. The sun is but a morning star."

"On the 29th of April . . . I was fishing from the bank of the river near the Nine-Acre-Corner bridge, standing on the quaking grass and willow roots, where the muskrats lurk . . ."

"It is remarkable how many creatures live wild and free though secret in the woods, and still sustain themselves in the neighborhood of towns, suspected by hunters only. . . . I formerly saw the raccoon in the woods behind where my house is built. . . ."

"All day long the red squirrels came and went, and afforded me much entertainment by their manoeuvres. . . . for all the motions of a squirrel, even in the most solitary recesses of the forest, imply spectators as much as those of a dancing girl . . ."

"Sometimes, when I pushed off my boat in the morning, I disturbed a great mud-turtle which had secreted himself under the boat in the night."

"As I stand over the insect crawling amid the pine needles on the forest floor, and endeavoring to conceal itself from my sight, and ask myself why it will cherish those humble thoughts, and hide its head from me who might, perhaps, be its benefactor, and impart to its race some cheering information, I am reminded of the greater Benefactor and Intelligence that stands over me the human insect."

[99]

"At a certain season of our life we are accustomed to consider every spot as the possible site of a house. I have thus surveyed the country on every side within a dozen miles of where I live. . . . The future inhabitants of this region, wherever they may place their houses, may be sure that they have been anticipated."

"A lake is the landscape's most beautiful and expressive feature. It is earth's eye; looking into which the beholder measures the depth of his own nature."

"In a pleasant spring morning all men's sins are forgiven. Such a day is a truce to vice. . . . Why the jailer does not leave open his prison doors — why the judge does not dismiss his case — why the preacher does not dismiss his congregation!"

"We are acquainted with a mere pellicle of the globe on which we live. Most have not delved six feet beneath the surface, nor leaped as many above it. We know not where we are. Beside, we are sound asleep nearly half our time. Yet we esteem ourselves wise, and have an established order on the surface."

". . . it is now dark . . . The wildest animals do not repose, but seek their prey now; the fox, and skunk, and rabbit, now roam the fields and woods without fear. They are Nature's watchmen — links which connect the days of animated life."

". . . all the shore rang with the trump of bullfrogs, the sturdy spirits of an-cient wine-bibbers and wassailers, still unrepentant, trying to sing a catch in their Stygian lake — if the Walden nymphs will pardon the comparison. . ."

"One attraction in coming to the woods to live was that I should have leisure and opportunity to see the Spring come in. . . . Fogs and rains and warmer suns are gradually melting the snow; the days have grown sensibly longer; and I see how I shall get through the winter without adding to my wood-pile, for large fires are no longer necessary."

"No yard! but unfenced nature reaching up to your very sills. . . . Instead of no path to the front-yard gate in the Great Snow — no gate — no front-yard — and no path to the civilized world."

"To be in company, even with the best, is soon wearisome and dissipating. I love to be alone. I never found the companion that was so companionable as solitude."

"In one direction from my house there was a colony of muskrats in the river meadows; under the grove of elms and buttonwoods in the other horizon was a village of busy men, as curious to me as if they had been prairie-dogs, each sitting at the mouth of its burrow, or running over to a neighbor's to gossip."

"The Fitchburg Railroad touches the pond about a hundred rods south of where I dwell. I usually go to the village along its causeway, and am, as it were, related to society by this link."

"I came to love my rows, my beans, though so many more than I wanted. They attached me to the earth, and so I got strength like Antaeus."

"While yet it is cold January, and snow and ice are thick and solid, the prudent landlord comes from the village to get ice to cool his summer drink; impressively, even pathetically, wise, to foresee the heat and thirst of July now in January . . . when so many things are not provided for."

". . . it was pleasant to compare the first tender signs of the infant year just peeping forth with the stately beauty of the withered vegetation which had withstood the winter . . . those unexhausted granaries which entertain the earliest birds — decent weeds, at least, which widowed Nature wears."

"The wasps came by thousands to my lodge in October, as to winter quarters, and settled on my windows within and on the walls overhead, sometimes deterring visitors from entering."

"God is alone — but the devil, he is far from being alone; he sees a great deal of company; he is legion. I am no more lonely than a single mullein or dandelion in a pasture, or a bean leaf, or sorrel, or a horse-fly, or a humblebee."

". . . when at length I had made one cast over the pickerelweed. . . . the thunder began to rumble. . . . The gods must be proud, thought I, with such forked flashes to rout a poor unarmed fisherman."

"The life in us is like the water in the river. It may rise this year higher than man has ever known it, and flood the parched uplands; even this may be the eventful year, which will drown out all our muskrats."

"Not long since I read his epitaph in the old Lincoln burying-ground, a little on one side, near the unmarked graves of some British grenadiers who fell in the retreat from Concord — where he is styled 'Sippio Brister' — Scipio Africanus he had some title to be called — 'a man of color,' as if he were discolored."

"Commonly I rested an hour or two in the shade at noon, after planting, and ate my lunch, and read a little by a spring which was the source of a swamp and of a brook, oozing from under Brister's Hill, half a mile from my field."

"When chestnuts were ripe I laid up half a bushel for winter. It was very exciting at that season to roam the then boundless chestnut woods of Lincoln — they now sleep their long sleep under the railroad — with a bag on my shoulder, and a stick to open burs with in my hand. . . ."

"The indescribable innocence and beneficence of Nature — of sun and wind and rain, of summer and winter — such health, such cheer, they afford forever! and such sympathy have they ever with our race . . ."

"In the morning I watched the geese from the door through the mist, sailing in the middle of the pond . . . But when I stood on the shore they at once rose up with a great flapping of wings at the signal of their commander. . . ."

"It is well to have some water in your neighborhood, to give buoyancy to and float the earth. One value even of the smallest well is, that when you look into it you see that earth is not continent but insular. This is as important as that it keeps butter cool."

"The first sparrow of spring! The year beginning with younger hope than ever! The faint silvery warblings heard above the partially bare and moist fields from the bluebird, the song sparrow, and the red-wing, as if the last flakes of winter tinkled as they fell!"

"Each morning the manager of this gallery substituted some new picture, distinguished by more brilliant or harmonious coloring, for the old upon the walls."

"The mice which haunted my house were not the common ones . . . but a wild native kind . . . When I was building, one of these had its nest underneath the house, and before I had laid the second floor . . . would come out regularly at lunch time and pick up the crumbs at my feet."

"Instead of calling on some scholar, I paid many a visit to particular trees . . . such as . . . a more perfect hemlock than usual, standing like a pagoda in the midst of the woods . . . These were the shrines I visited both summer and winter."

"Many of the phenomena of Winter are suggestive of an inexpressible tenderness and fragile delicacy. We are accustomed to hear this king described as a rude and boisterous tyrant; but with the gentleness of a lover he adorns the tresses of Summer."

"That man who does not believe that each day contains an earlier, more sacred, and auroral hour than he has yet profaned, has despaired of life, and is pursuing a descending and darkening way."

". . . the blue flag grows thinly in the pure water, rising from the stony bottom all around the shore, where it is visited by hummingbirds in June; and the color both of its bluish blades and its flowers and especially their reflections, is in singular harmony with the glaucous water."

"If the day and the night are such that you greet them with joy, and life emits a fragrance like flowers and sweet-scented herbs, is more elastic, more starry, more immortal — that is your success. All nature is your congratulation, and you have cause momentarily to bless yourself."

"I left the woods for as good a reason as I went there. Perhaps it seemed to me that I had several more lives to live, and could not spare any more time for that one."

"I learned this, at least, by my experiment: that if one advances confidently in the direction of his dreams, and endeavors to live the life which he has imagined, he will meet with a success unexpected in common hours."

For those who may wish to know the exact locations of some of the scenes depicted on these pages, the following information will supplement that given on the map.

PRINTER'S NOTE

This book has been printed and bound by The Plimpton Press, Norwood, Massachusetts. The half-tone printing plates were made by Walker Engraving Company, New York.

The end-paper map, the drawing of Thoreau, the photographs, and the general plan of the book are by Mr. Kane. The binding scheme is based on original designs by W. A. Dwiggins. The typography of the book is by James Hendrickson.